Fuck Your Gratitude

Copyright © 2020 Kooky Rosso Press

DAY: M T W T F S S   DATE 09/09

Asshole Of The Day Award Goes To....
My BOSS

Let Out The Rage... Doodle/Stick Here!

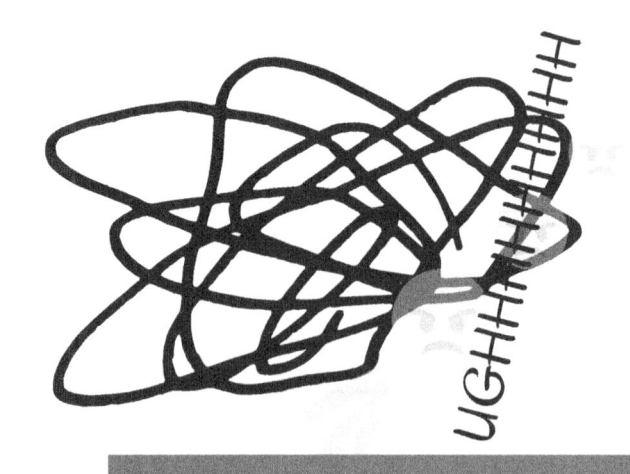

UGHHHHHHHHH

EXAMPLE

You're Feeling? Circle One!

Three Things That SUCKED Today:

1. My BOSSSSSSS!!!!!!

2. Stupid woman on the train!

3. My CAT pooped on the floor!

Shit I must remember:

- ☐ Meal plan
- ☐ Go for run
- ☐ Catch up with kay
- ☐ Be gratfeul!
- ☐ Stop being a bitch

Shit I must FORGET:

I really want to forget that I cried in my office today!

I give zero fucks ~~about~~ what people ~~think~~ (Or that's my aim).

TOMORROW I will....

Be calm and collected! Be an amazing employee!

A Positive End: The Best Bit About Today?

I went on a long walk in the woods nearby... it made me feel so much better being out in nature. Erm... Also, my caramel coffee this morning was AMAZING!

TOMORROW WILL BE BETTER!!

EXAMPLE

DAY: M T W T F S S   DATE _____

Asshole Of The Day Award Goes To....
_____

Let Out The Rage... Doodle Here!

You're Feeling? Circle One!

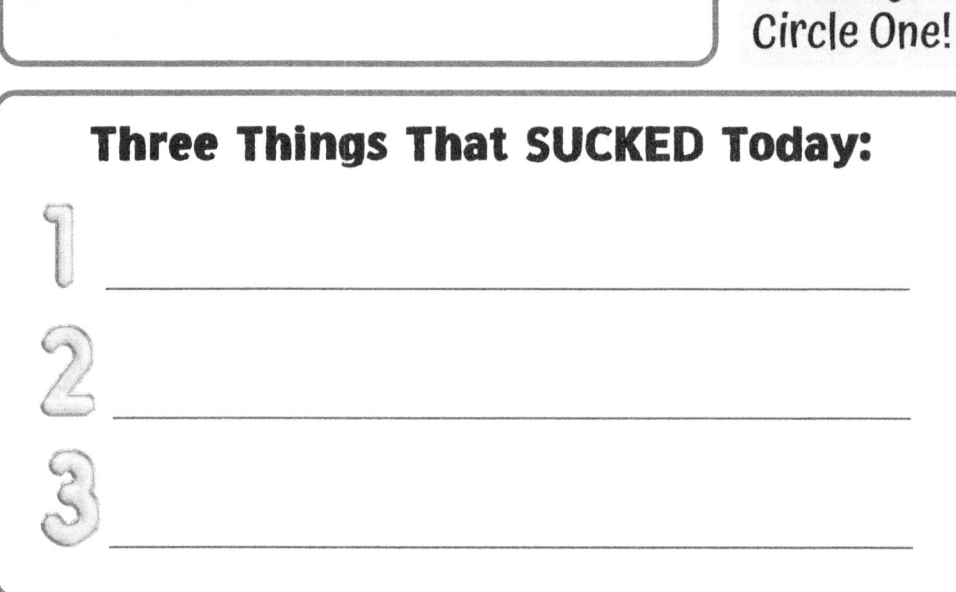

Three Things That SUCKED Today:

1. _____
2. _____
3. _____

Shit I must remember:	Shit I must FORGET:
○ _____ ○ _____ ○ _____ ○ _____ ○ _____	
I give zero fucks about:	**TOMORROW I will....**

A Positive End: The Best Bit About Today?

DAY: M T W T F S S   DATE _____

Asshole Of The Day Award Goes To....
_____

Let Out The Rage... Doodle Here!

You're Feeling? Circle One!

Three Things That SUCKED Today:

1. _____
2. _____
3. _____

Shit I must remember:

- _____
- _____
- _____
- _____
- _____

Shit I must FORGET:

I give zero fucks about:

TOMORROW I will....

A Positive End: The Best Bit About Today?

DAY: M T W T F S S   DATE _____

Asshole Of The Day Award Goes To....
_____

Let Out The Rage... Doodle Here!

You're Feeling? Circle One!

Three Things That SUCKED Today:

1. _____
2. _____
3. _____

Shit I must remember:	Shit I must FORGET:
○ _____	
○ _____	
○ _____	
○ _____	
○ _____	

I give zero fucks about:	TOMORROW I will....

A Positive End: The Best Bit About Today?

DAY: M T W T F S S   DATE _____

Asshole Of The Day Award Goes To....
_____

Let Out The Rage... Doodle Here!

You're Feeling? Circle One!

Three Things That SUCKED Today:

1. _____
2. _____
3. _____

Shit I must remember:	Shit I must FORGET:
○ _____ ○ _____ ○ _____ ○ _____ ○ _____	
I give zero fucks about:	**TOMORROW I will....**

A Positive End: The Best Bit About Today?

DAY: M T W T F S S   DATE _____

Asshole Of The Day Award Goes To....
_____

Let Out The Rage... Doodle Here!

You're Feeling? Circle One!

Three Things That SUCKED Today:

1. _____
2. _____
3. _____

Shit I must remember:

- _____
- _____
- _____
- _____
- _____

Shit I must FORGET:

I give zero fucks about:

TOMORROW I will....

A Positive End: The Best Bit About Today?

DAY: M T W T F S S   DATE _____

Asshole Of The Day Award Goes To....
_____

Let Out The Rage... Doodle Here!

You're Feeling? Circle One!

Three Things That SUCKED Today:

1. _____
2. _____
3. _____

Shit I must remember:	Shit I must FORGET:
○ _____ ○ _____ ○ _____ ○ _____ ○ _____	
I give zero fucks about:	TOMORROW I will....

A Positive End: The Best Bit About Today?

DAY: M T W T F S S DATE _____

Asshole Of The Day Award Goes To....
_____

Let Out The Rage... Doodle Here!

You're Feeling? Circle One!

Three Things That SUCKED Today:

1 _____
2 _____
3 _____

Shit I must remember:
- _____
- _____
- _____
- _____
- _____

Shit I must FORGET:

I give zero fucks about:

TOMORROW I will....

A Positive End: The Best Bit About Today?

DAY: M T W T F S S   DATE _____

Asshole Of The Day Award Goes To....
_____

Let Out The Rage... Doodle Here!

You're Feeling? Circle One!

Three Things That SUCKED Today:

1. _____
2. _____
3. _____

Shit I must remember:

- _____
- _____
- _____
- _____
- _____

Shit I must FORGET:

I give zero fucks about:

TOMORROW I will....

A Positive End: The Best Bit About Today?

DAY: M T W T F S S   DATE _____

Asshole Of The Day Award Goes To....
_____

Let Out The Rage... Doodle Here!

You're Feeling? Circle One!

Three Things That SUCKED Today:

1. _____
2. _____
3. _____

Shit I must remember:	Shit I must FORGET:
○ _____	
○ _____	
○ _____	
○ _____	
○ _____	

I give zero fucks about:	TOMORROW I will....

A Positive End: The Best Bit About Today?

DAY: M T W T F S S   DATE _____

Asshole Of The Day Award Goes To....
_____

Let Out The Rage... Doodle Here!

You're Feeling? Circle One!

Three Things That SUCKED Today:

1. _____
2. _____
3. _____

Shit I must remember:	Shit I must FORGET:
○ _____ ○ _____ ○ _____ ○ _____ ○ _____	
I give zero fucks about:	TOMORROW I will....

A Positive End: The Best Bit About Today?

DAY: M T W T F S S   DATE _____

Asshole Of The Day Award Goes To....
_____

Let Out The Rage... Doodle Here!

You're Feeling? Circle One!

Three Things That SUCKED Today:

1. _____
2. _____
3. _____

Shit I must remember:	Shit I must FORGET:
○ _____	
○ _____	
○ _____	
○ _____	
○ _____	

I give zero fucks about:	TOMORROW I will....

A Positive End: The Best Bit About Today?

DAY: M T W T F S S   DATE _____

Asshole Of The Day Award Goes To....
_____

Let Out The Rage... Doodle Here!

You're Feeling? Circle One!

Three Things That SUCKED Today:

1. _____
2. _____
3. _____

Shit I must remember: ○ _____ ○ _____ ○ _____ ○ _____ ○ _____	**Shit I must FORGET:**
I give zero fucks about:	**TOMORROW I will....**

A Positive End: The Best Bit About Today?

DAY: M T W T F S S   DATE _____

Asshole Of The Day Award Goes To....
_____

Let Out The Rage... Doodle Here!

You're Feeling? Circle One!

Three Things That SUCKED Today:

1. _____
2. _____
3. _____

Shit I must remember:

- _____
- _____
- _____
- _____
- _____

Shit I must FORGET:

I give zero fucks about:

TOMORROW I will....

A Positive End: The Best Bit About Today?

DAY: M T W T F S S   DATE _____

Asshole Of The Day Award Goes To....
_____

Let Out The Rage... Doodle Here!

You're Feeling? Circle One!

Three Things That SUCKED Today:

1. _____
2. _____
3. _____

Shit I must remember:

- _____
- _____
- _____
- _____
- _____

Shit I must FORGET:

I give zero fucks about:

TOMORROW I will....

A Positive End: The Best Bit About Today?

DAY: M T W T F S S   DATE _____

Asshole Of The Day Award Goes To....
_____

Let Out The Rage... Doodle Here!

You're Feeling? Circle One!

Three Things That SUCKED Today:

1. _____
2. _____
3. _____

Shit I must remember:	Shit I must FORGET:
○ _____ ○ _____ ○ _____ ○ _____ ○ _____	
I give zero fucks about:	**TOMORROW I will....**

A Positive End: The Best Bit About Today?

DAY: M T W T F S S   DATE _____

Asshole Of The Day Award Goes To....
_____

Let Out The Rage... Doodle Here!

You're Feeling? Circle One!

Three Things That SUCKED Today:

1. _____
2. _____
3. _____

Shit I must remember:	Shit I must FORGET:
○ _____	
○ _____	
○ _____	
○ _____	
○ _____	

I give zero fucks about:	TOMORROW I will....

A Positive End: The Best Bit About Today?

DAY: M T W T F S S   DATE _____

Asshole Of The Day Award Goes To....
_____

Let Out The Rage... Doodle Here!

You're Feeling? Circle One!

Three Things That SUCKED Today:

1. _____
2. _____
3. _____

Shit I must remember:	Shit I must FORGET:
○ _____ ○ _____ ○ _____ ○ _____ ○ _____	

I give zero fucks about:	TOMORROW I will….

A Positive End: The Best Bit About Today?

DAY: M T W T F S S   DATE _____

Asshole Of The Day Award Goes To....
_____

Let Out The Rage... Doodle Here!

You're Feeling? Circle One!

Three Things That SUCKED Today:

1. _____
2. _____
3. _____

Shit I must remember:

- _____
- _____
- _____
- _____
- _____

Shit I must FORGET:

I give zero fucks about:

TOMORROW I will....

A Positive End: The Best Bit About Today?

DAY: M T W T F S S   DATE _____

Asshole Of The Day Award Goes To....
_____

Let Out The Rage... Doodle Here!

You're Feeling? Circle One!

Three Things That SUCKED Today:

1 _____
2 _____
3 _____

Shit I must remember:	Shit I must FORGET:
○ _____	
○ _____	
○ _____	
○ _____	
○ _____	

I give zero fucks about:	TOMORROW I will....

A Positive End: The Best Bit About Today?

DAY: M T W T F S S   DATE _____

Asshole Of The Day Award Goes To....
_____

Let Out The Rage... Doodle Here!

You're Feeling? Circle One!

Three Things That SUCKED Today:

1. _____
2. _____
3. _____

Shit I must remember:
- _____
- _____
- _____
- _____
- _____

Shit I must FORGET:

I give zero fucks about:

TOMORROW I will....

A Positive End: The Best Bit About Today?

DAY: M T W T F S S   DATE _____

Asshole Of The Day Award Goes To....
_____

Let Out The Rage... Doodle Here!

You're Feeling? Circle One!

Three Things That SUCKED Today:

1. _____
2. _____
3. _____

Shit I must remember:	Shit I must FORGET:
○ _____ ○ _____ ○ _____ ○ _____ ○ _____	
I give zero fucks about:	**TOMORROW I will....**

A Positive End: The Best Bit About Today?

_____

_____

_____

_____

DAY: M T W T F S S   DATE _____

Asshole Of The Day Award Goes To....
_____

Let Out The Rage... Doodle Here!

You're Feeling? Circle One!

Three Things That SUCKED Today:

1. _____
2. _____
3. _____

Shit I must remember:
- _____
- _____
- _____
- _____
- _____

Shit I must FORGET:

I give zero fucks about:

TOMORROW I will....

A Positive End: The Best Bit About Today?

DAY: M T W T F S S DATE _____

Asshole Of The Day Award Goes To....
_____

Let Out The Rage... Doodle Here!

You're Feeling? Circle One!

Three Things That SUCKED Today:

1. _____
2. _____
3. _____

Shit I must remember:	Shit I must FORGET:
○ _____ ○ _____ ○ _____ ○ _____ ○ _____	|file
I give zero fucks about:	**TOMORROW I will....**

A Positive End: The Best Bit About Today?

DAY: M T W T F S S   DATE _____

Asshole Of The Day Award Goes To....
_____

Let Out The Rage... Doodle Here!

You're Feeling? Circle One!

Three Things That SUCKED Today:

1. _____
2. _____
3. _____

Shit I must remember:	Shit I must FORGET:
○ _____	
○ _____	
○ _____	
○ _____	
○ _____	

I give zero fucks about:	TOMORROW I will....

A Positive End: The Best Bit About Today?

DAY: M T W T F S S   DATE _____

Asshole Of The Day Award Goes To....
_____

Let Out The Rage... Doodle Here!

You're Feeling? Circle One!

Three Things That SUCKED Today:

1. _____
2. _____
3. _____

Shit I must remember:	Shit I must FORGET:
○ _____	
○ _____	
○ _____	
○ _____	
○ _____	

I give zero fucks about:	TOMORROW I will....

A Positive End: The Best Bit About Today?

DAY: M T W T F S S   DATE _____

Asshole Of The Day Award Goes To....
_____

Let Out The Rage... Doodle Here!

You're Feeling? Circle One!

Three Things That SUCKED Today:

1 _____

2 _____

3 _____

Shit I must remember:	Shit I must FORGET:
○ _____	
○ _____	
○ _____	
○ _____	
○ _____	

I give zero fucks about:	TOMORROW I will....

A Positive End: The Best Bit About Today?

DAY: M T W T F S S   DATE _____

Asshole Of The Day Award Goes To....
_____

Let Out The Rage... Doodle Here!

You're Feeling? Circle One!

Three Things That SUCKED Today:

1. _____
2. _____
3. _____

Shit I must remember:	Shit I must FORGET:
○ _____	
○ _____	
○ _____	
○ _____	
○ _____	

I give zero fucks about:	TOMORROW I will....

A Positive End: The Best Bit About Today?

DAY: M T W T F S S   DATE _____

Asshole Of The Day Award Goes To....
_____

Let Out The Rage... Doodle Here!

You're Feeling? Circle One!

Three Things That SUCKED Today:

1. _____
2. _____
3. _____

Shit I must remember:

- _____
- _____
- _____
- _____
- _____

Shit I must FORGET:

I give zero fucks about:

TOMORROW I will....

A Positive End: The Best Bit About Today?

DAY: M T W T F S S   DATE _____

Asshole Of The Day Award Goes To....
_____

Let Out The Rage... Doodle Here!

You're Feeling? Circle One!

Three Things That SUCKED Today:

1. _____
2. _____
3. _____

Shit I must remember:	Shit I must FORGET:
○ _____	
○ _____	
○ _____	
○ _____	
○ _____	

I give zero fucks about:	TOMORROW I will....

A Positive End: The Best Bit About Today?

DAY: M T W T F S S   DATE _____

Asshole Of The Day Award Goes To....
_____

Let Out The Rage... Doodle Here!

You're Feeling? Circle One!

Three Things That SUCKED Today:

1. _____
2. _____
3. _____

Shit I must remember:	Shit I must FORGET:
○ _____ ○ _____ ○ _____ ○ _____ ○ _____	
I give zero fucks about:	**TOMORROW I will....**

A Positive End: The Best Bit About Today?

_____

_____

_____

_____

DAY: M T W T F S S   DATE _____

Asshole Of The Day Award Goes To....
_____

Let Out The Rage... Doodle Here!

You're Feeling? Circle One!

Three Things That SUCKED Today:

1. _____
2. _____
3. _____

Shit I must remember:	Shit I must FORGET:
○ _____	
○ _____	
○ _____	
○ _____	
○ _____	

I give zero fucks about:	TOMORROW I will....

A Positive End: The Best Bit About Today?

DAY: M T W T F S S   DATE _____

Asshole Of The Day Award Goes To....
_____

Let Out The Rage... Doodle Here!

You're Feeling? Circle One!

Three Things That SUCKED Today:

1. _____
2. _____
3. _____

Shit I must remember:	Shit I must FORGET:
○ _____	
○ _____	
○ _____	
○ _____	
○ _____	

I give zero fucks about:	TOMORROW I will....

A Positive End: The Best Bit About Today?

DAY: M T W T F S S   DATE _____

Asshole Of The Day Award Goes To....
_____

Let Out The Rage... Doodle Here!

You're Feeling? Circle One!

Three Things That SUCKED Today:

1. _____
2. _____
3. _____

Shit I must remember:

- _____
- _____
- _____
- _____
- _____

Shit I must FORGET:

I give zero fucks about:

TOMORROW I will....

A Positive End: The Best Bit About Today?

DAY: M T W T F S S   DATE _____

Asshole Of The Day Award Goes To....
_____

Let Out The Rage... Doodle Here!

You're Feeling? Circle One!

Three Things That SUCKED Today:

1. _____
2. _____
3. _____

Shit I must remember:

- _____
- _____
- _____
- _____
- _____

Shit I must FORGET:

I give zero fucks about:

TOMORROW I will....

A Positive End: The Best Bit About Today?

DAY: M T W T F S S   DATE _____

Asshole Of The Day Award Goes To....
_____

Let Out The Rage... Doodle Here!

You're Feeling? Circle One!

Three Things That SUCKED Today:

1. _____
2. _____
3. _____

Shit I must remember:	Shit I must FORGET:
○ _____	
○ _____	
○ _____	
○ _____	
○ _____	

I give zero fucks about:	TOMORROW I will....

A Positive End: The Best Bit About Today?

DAY: M T W T F S S   DATE _____

Asshole Of The Day Award Goes To....
_____

Let Out The Rage... Doodle Here!

You're Feeling? Circle One!

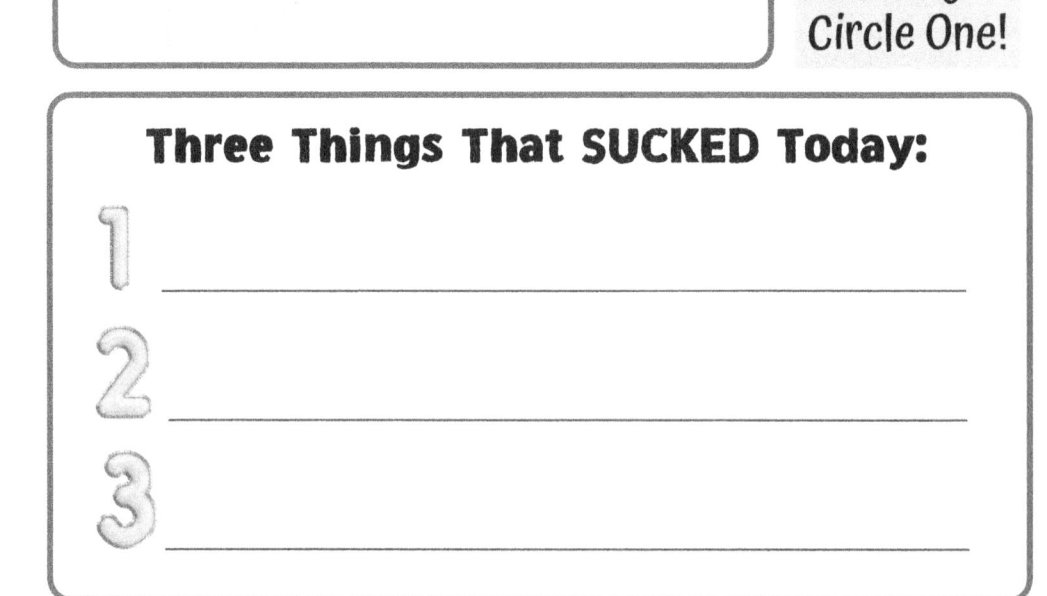

Three Things That SUCKED Today:

1 _____

2 _____

3 _____

Shit I must remember:

○ _____
○ _____
○ _____
○ _____
○ _____

Shit I must FORGET:

I give zero fucks about:

TOMORROW I will....

A Positive End: The Best Bit About Today?

DAY: M T W T F S S   DATE _____

Asshole Of The Day Award Goes To....
_____

Let Out The Rage... Doodle Here!

You're Feeling? Circle One!

Three Things That SUCKED Today:

1. _____
2. _____
3. _____

Shit I must remember:	Shit I must FORGET:
○ _____ ○ _____ ○ _____ ○ _____ ○ _____	
I give zero fucks about:	TOMORROW I will....

A Positive End: The Best Bit About Today?

DAY: M T W T F S S   DATE _____

Asshole Of The Day Award Goes To....
_____

Let Out The Rage... Doodle Here!

You're Feeling? Circle One!

Three Things That SUCKED Today:

1. _____
2. _____
3. _____

Shit I must remember:	Shit I must FORGET:
○ _____	
○ _____	
○ _____	
○ _____	
○ _____	

I give zero fucks about:	TOMORROW I will....

A Positive End: The Best Bit About Today?

DAY: M T W T F S S   DATE _____

Asshole Of The Day Award Goes To....
_____

Let Out The Rage... Doodle Here!

You're Feeling? Circle One!

Three Things That SUCKED Today:

1. _____
2. _____
3. _____

Shit I must remember:	Shit I must FORGET:
○ _____ ○ _____ ○ _____ ○ _____ ○ _____	

I give zero fucks about:	TOMORROW I will....

A Positive End: The Best Bit About Today?

DAY: M T W T F S S   DATE _____

Asshole Of The Day Award Goes To....
_____

Let Out The Rage... Doodle Here!

You're Feeling? Circle One!

Three Things That SUCKED Today:

1. _____
2. _____
3. _____

Shit I must remember:	Shit I must FORGET:
○ _____ ○ _____ ○ _____ ○ _____ ○ _____	
I give zero fucks about:	TOMORROW I will....

A Positive End: The Best Bit About Today?

DAY: M T W T F S S   DATE _____

Asshole Of The Day Award Goes To....
_____

Let Out The Rage... Doodle Here!

You're Feeling? Circle One!

Three Things That SUCKED Today:

1. _____
2. _____
3. _____

Shit I must remember:	Shit I must FORGET:
○ _____	
○ _____	
○ _____	
○ _____	
○ _____	

I give zero fucks about:	TOMORROW I will....

A Positive End: The Best Bit About Today?

DAY: M T W T F S S   DATE _____

Asshole Of The Day Award Goes To....
_____

Let Out The Rage... Doodle Here!

You're Feeling? Circle One!

Three Things That SUCKED Today:

1. _____
2. _____
3. _____

Shit I must remember:	Shit I must FORGET:
○ _____ ○ _____ ○ _____ ○ _____ ○ _____	

I give zero fucks about:	TOMORROW I will....

A Positive End: The Best Bit About Today?

DAY: M T W T F S S DATE _____

Asshole Of The Day Award Goes To....
_____

Let Out The Rage... Doodle Here!

You're Feeling? Circle One!

Three Things That SUCKED Today:

1. _____
2. _____
3. _____

Shit I must remember:	Shit I must FORGET:
○ _____	
○ _____	
○ _____	
○ _____	
○ _____	

I give zero fucks about:	TOMORROW I will....

A Positive End: The Best Bit About Today?

DAY: M T W T F S S DATE _____

Asshole Of The Day Award Goes To....
_____

Let Out The Rage... Doodle Here!

You're Feeling? Circle One!

Three Things That SUCKED Today:

1. _____
2. _____
3. _____

Shit I must remember:	Shit I must FORGET:
○ _____	
○ _____	
○ _____	
○ _____	
○ _____	

I give zero fucks about:	TOMORROW I will....

A Positive End: The Best Bit About Today?

DAY: M T W T F S S DATE _____

Asshole Of The Day Award Goes To....
_____

Let Out The Rage... Doodle Here!

You're Feeling? Circle One!

Three Things That SUCKED Today:

1. _____
2. _____
3. _____

Shit I must remember:	Shit I must FORGET:
○ _____ ○ _____ ○ _____ ○ _____ ○ _____	

I give zero fucks about:	TOMORROW I will....

A Positive End: The Best Bit About Today?

DAY: M T W T F S S   DATE _____

Asshole Of The Day Award Goes To....
_____

Let Out The Rage... Doodle Here!

You're Feeling? Circle One!

Three Things That SUCKED Today:

1. _____
2. _____
3. _____

Shit I must remember:	Shit I must FORGET:
○ _____	
○ _____	
○ _____	
○ _____	
○ _____	

I give zero fucks about:	TOMORROW I will....

A Positive End: The Best Bit About Today?

DAY: M T W T F S S   DATE _____

Asshole Of The Day Award Goes To....

_____

Let Out The Rage... Doodle Here!

You're Feeling? Circle One!

Three Things That SUCKED Today:

1. _____
2. _____
3. _____

Shit I must remember:	Shit I must FORGET:
○ _____	
○ _____	
○ _____	
○ _____	
○ _____	

I give zero fucks about:	TOMORROW I will....

A Positive End: The Best Bit About Today?

DAY: M T W T F S S   DATE _____

Asshole Of The Day Award Goes To....
_____

Let Out The Rage... Doodle Here!

You're Feeling? Circle One!

Three Things That SUCKED Today:

1. _____
2. _____
3. _____

Shit I must remember:	Shit I must FORGET:
○ _____ ○ _____ ○ _____ ○ _____ ○ _____	

I give zero fucks about:	TOMORROW I will....

A Positive End: The Best Bit About Today?

DAY: M T W T F S S   DATE _____

Asshole Of The Day Award Goes To....
_____

Let Out The Rage... Doodle Here!

You're Feeling? Circle One!

Three Things That SUCKED Today:

1. _____
2. _____
3. _____

Shit I must remember:	Shit I must FORGET:
○ _____ ○ _____ ○ _____ ○ _____ ○ _____	

I give zero fucks about:	TOMORROW I will....

A Positive End: The Best Bit About Today?

DAY: M T W T F S S   DATE _____

Asshole Of The Day Award Goes To....
_____

Let Out The Rage... Doodle Here!

You're Feeling? Circle One!

Three Things That SUCKED Today:

1 _____

2 _____

3 _____

Shit I must remember:	Shit I must FORGET:
○ _____ ○ _____ ○ _____ ○ _____ ○ _____	

I give zero fucks about:	TOMORROW I will....

A Positive End: The Best Bit About Today?

DAY: M T W T F S S   DATE _____

Asshole Of The Day Award Goes To....
_____

Let Out The Rage... Doodle Here!

You're Feeling? Circle One!

Three Things That SUCKED Today:

1. _____
2. _____
3. _____

Shit I must remember:	Shit I must FORGET:
○ _____	
○ _____	
○ _____	
○ _____	
○ _____	

I give zero fucks about:	TOMORROW I will....

A Positive End: The Best Bit About Today?

DAY: M T W T F S S   DATE _____

Asshole Of The Day Award Goes To....
_____

Let Out The Rage... Doodle Here!

You're Feeling? Circle One!

Three Things That SUCKED Today:

1 _____
2 _____
3 _____

Shit I must remember:	Shit I must FORGET:
○ _____	
○ _____	
○ _____	
○ _____	
○ _____	

I give zero fucks about:	TOMORROW I will....

A Positive End: The Best Bit About Today?

Made in the USA
Monee, IL
19 March 2024